All This Stress

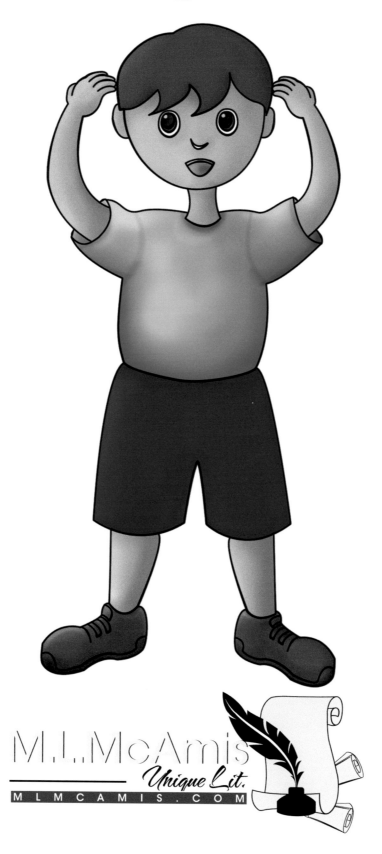

M.L.McAmis
Unique Lit.
MLMCAMIS.COM

I opened my eyes and there was Momma. She was in her house coat smiling at me. She kissed me on the head and said, "My little sweetheart, it is time to get up De-Stress."

I pushed back my covers. I then put my feet in my bunny slippers. I slowly stood up and walked to my window.

I saw cars pulling out of driveways. People were walking to their mailboxes to put mail in. Women were watering their flowers. All of them seemed to be in a hurry.

I slowly shook my head side to side. I put my hands on my head, blinked my eyes and said, "I just can't handle all this stress."

I quickly ran back to bed. I threw my bunny slippers on the floor and pulled the covers over my head. I was hiding from all of that stressful stuff.

I thought that I could stay safely snuggled in my warm bed. All that stressful stuff couldn't get to me and make me grouchy and have a headache like Momma and Daddy talk about.

Then I heard Momma laughing as she came back into my room. She gently pulled the cover off my head and sat down beside me. She hugged me tightly and kissed my cheek. She said, "It'll be o.k. De-Stress."

I felt much better when she told me that. I smiled, hugged her, and said, "O.k., Momma."

She put my bunny slippers back on my feet and covered my cold toes. I moved my feet around and made the bunny ears flop and we both laughed.

Holding Momma's hand I slowly slipped out of bed and put my feet on the floor. Her and I walked toward the door.

Momma walked me into the bathroom and turned on the water in the sink for me to wash my hands. I reached and put my little fingers around the soap. I spun it around and around and washed my hands.

I then rinsed my hands and looked around for my mom, but she wasn't there. I looked around and shook my head side to side. It was o.k. though. I said, "I'll be o.k." I dried my hands on the towel.

I started out of the bathroom and wham! I was almost knocked down by an armful of laundry. Momma was in a hurry. Mom said, "I am sorry De-Stress. I have to get this laundry started before breakfast."

She reached in the hamper and grabbed up the clothes and off she went down the hall. I looked down and she had dropped a pair of Dad's bloomers. Ha, ha, ha, that was funny.

I picked up the bloomers and quickly ran down the hall to give them to Mom. As I went by the kitchen Dad yelled, "Slow down De-Stress."

I said, "Hi Daddy. I have to get these to Momma and see if she can get this brown stain out of them."

Daddy laughed when I was running to Momma with the bloomers. I held them out and gave them to Momma and she laughed. She put them in the washing machine, put some stuff in, and turned it on.

She had the door of the dryer open and I looked in. She pulled a fabric softener sheet from the box and was turning those buttons. She pushed one of the buttons and then was doing something else. She turned it off and pulled something from the top of it.

I slowly shook my head side to side, gently raised my hands to the top of my head and said, "I just can't handle all this stress!"

I heard Dad laughing as he walked down the hall. He stuck his head into my room and said, "Come on De-Stress."

I pulled my covers down and said, "Come here Dad."

He picked my slippers up, sat on the end of my bed and said, "De-Stress, everything will be o.k. I promise. "

I sat up, put my slippers back on and said, "It'll all be o.k." I slowly shook my head side to side as I got out of bed.

He and I walked to the table and he pulled out my chair. I climbed up in it and sat down. I watched mom at the stove. She was still working very hard it seemed. I heard Dad saying that he would have to wait until next week to pay the cable. Mom told him that would be o.k. Then she started talking about paying something else and they started arguing.

I gently started shaking my head. I slowly put my hands on my head and said, "I can't handle all this stress."

I then climbed under the table with my hands over my ears and shut my eyes. I sat there for just a little bit and was really getting stressed out.

My mom put her head under one side of the table and Dad put his head under the table on the other side. Both of them told me that it would be o.k. They smiled at me.

I crawled out from under the table and back into my chair. My breakfast was ready to eat now. I started off with a piece of bacon. Then I picked up my spoon and ate some of my cereal.

It seemed like everything was o.k. I finished eating my breakfast. I was ready to go to the bathroom and brush my teeth. I looked at my teeth with the bubbles.

I gently squeezed the toothpaste onto my brush and started to brush. Up and down then side to side till I got all my teeth brushed.

I ran some water into my cup. I sloshed it around in my mouth and rinsed. I washed my face off a little with my hands and dried with the towel.

I put on the clothes that Mom had hung on the hanger. I was ready for school. Mom held my hand and walked me to the end of the sidewalk to wait for the bus.

"There it comes around the corner. It will be here in a little bit," Momma said. "It will be here in just a little bit. It is getting closer."

The bus stopped in front of me and the doors came open. I slowly shook my head side to side as I looked up those steps going on the bus. I heard all those kids laughing and talking. I looked slowly up at my mom and put my hands on my head and said, "I just can't handle all this stress."

My mom hugged me and said, "It will be o.k. De-Stress. Your day will go by fast son."

That comforted me. I walked up the steps and sat down on the front seat. Just a little while later it was time to get off the bus and go into school.

I walked slowly toward the school. I looked side to side. Some of the kids I knew said, "Hi De-Stress."

There were a lot of kids. Some were running. Some were walking. There were big kids, little kids, parents, teachers, and cars that kids were getting out of.

I started up the stairs and into the door. I walked down the hall to my home room. I liked my teacher. She was nice to me. She always said, "Good morning De-Stress." She helped me handle all the stress at school. She helped me learn a lot.

I liked school. Most of the time I didn't get stressed out while I was there. Sometimes I did, though, when the older ones bullied me.

When I walked into the lunch room I saw all those kids. There was a long lunch line and I heard all those kids talking. I had to worry about milk, cool aid, or whatever I was going to drink. Then I had to decide which food I would eat. Sometimes I slowly blinked my eyes and shook my head side to side. I raised my hands to my head and said, "I just can't handle all this stress."

The lunch ladies always helped me in that predicament, though. They laughed and said, "It's o.k. De-Stress. Take your time and tell us what you want to eat today."

There was gym class also. That was rough sometimes, but I liked gym class, I enjoyed playing ball, and running, and playing other games.

I liked recess time. We had a nice playground. I liked the swings and the slide. Sometimes the kids wanted me to do things that I could get hurt doing, though. Some of them went down the slide head first. When they did that, I slowly shook my head side to side, put my hands on my head and said, "I just can't handle all this stress."

My teacher told me that it would be o.k. I could get hurt doing some of that. Then the ones that did it got in trouble.

By the end of the day I was always ready to go home. My teacher took our class down the hall. She helped us find our bus.

When I got on my bus, I usually sat on the front seat where I could see out. I liked being able to see out the front of the bus. I liked my bus driver too. He always said, " Hi De-Stress and bye De-Stress."

My Momma was always waiting for me when I got home. She always smiled and said, "Hi De-Stress." She hugged me and gave me a kiss on the cheek.

I sat at the supper table with Momma and Daddy and came up with a great plan. We needed somewhere to go to hide from all the stress that bothered us all the time.

Daddy talked about all the bills and things like he always did. Momma got up and down from the table getting butter, ketchup, and other things. I tried to decide if I wanted a bite of my mashed potatoes or my creamed corn. I began shaking my head slowly side to side. I raised my hands slowly to the top of my head and said, "I just can't handle all this stress."

I got out of my chair and ran down the hall. I pushed my bedroom door open and ran from all that stress. I climbed under my cover. I was careful not to get my shoes on the bed, though. Momma would fuss at me for having my shoes on the bed.

It wasn't long until Momma was sitting beside me on the bed and said, "It's o.k. De-Stress."

I pushed my cover back and told Momma that her and Daddy could borrow my blanket to hide under to hide from all the stress. She laughed and told me they would need a bigger blanket to hide from all their stress.

That got me thinking. I sat out to build my Momma and Daddy a place to hide from all the stress. I opened my toy box and went through it. I found a few things that I could use. I put them in the middle of the floor. I thought, Momma said they needed a bigger place to hide from stress. I opened my closet door and looked up in the top. There was a comforter in the top of the closet, but how would I get it down?

I went and got Momma. When she got to my room she saw all the toys in the floor. She said, "What are you doing De-Stress?"

I said, "It is a secret. I will tell you later." Then I said, "Will you get me the comforter from the top of the closet?"

She got the comforter down for me and asked if I needed anything else. I told her that I didn't need anything else right then but maybe in a little while.

I was thinking. Momma and Daddy won't come to my room to relieve stress, but they go to the front room for long periods of time. I will build their stress reliever in the front room.

I peeped out of my door, oops! Dad was standing in his room. I shut my door quietly. I sat there for a little bit, then I peeped out again.

There was no sign of Momma or Daddy. I quietly got the things and ran to the front room. I climbed up on the couch and put the comforter on top. I put a few toys under there too.

Oh no, I heard one of them coming down the hall. What was I to do? I got down off the couch. I thought, maybe I will go under the coffee table. I will go in the closet. They were coming. I slowly shook my head side to side. I put my hands on my head and said, "I just can't handle all this stress."

Dad said, "Are you o.k. De-Stress?"

I told him and Momma what I had done for them. They really liked the stress relief place that I built. They went there a lot too. They thanked me for building it. I think Momma and Daddy needed that place to get away from all the stress.

To order additional copies of this book, contact:
Xlibris
844-714-8691
www.Xlibris.com
Orders@Xlibris.com

ISBN: Softcover   978-1-6698-6491-2
         EBook   978-1-6698-6490-5

Library of Congress Control Number: 2023905927

Print information available on the last page

Rev. date: 01/31/2023

Printed in the United States
by Baker & Taylor Publisher Services